I Won't Apologize For What I'm About To Say…

I Won't Apologize For What I'm About To Say…

by

Martine Ashley

First Edition: [September 2021]
Printed in the United States of America
ISBN: [9781637905227]

Speak your truth unapologetically.
Your voice, your truth, and your pain are real.
They deserve to be heard.

You want the world to know you silenced me?
You want the world to know you used me at your convenience?
Whenever you rang the bell, I came running like a fool for you.
You want the world to know the power you carried over me?
Let's tell the world.
But will you tell the world your failed pursuits to boost your ego at my expense as well?
Will you tell the world those insecurities you assumed would disappear if you projected them onto me enough are still there?
Louder than ever,
Suffocating you little by little,
Making it harder for you to breathe with every breath you take.
Will you tell the world how frightened a woman's strength and confidence made such a strong manly man?
You want the recognition for destroying me?
Maybe consider including the fact that you were never whole to begin with; there has to be reasoning for wanting such a recognition, right?
Or maybe just maybe you parade around like you're this macho of a man, but you're just a scared child who collects woman's hearts in attempt to mask your failures as a man.

Recognition.

"Hold me down" he says.
"While I find myself."
but you won't stop cheating.
"Stop being selfish. can't you
see I'm finding myself babe?"

I stay.

"Hold me down" he says
"While I work on me."
but you're causing me pain.
"It's not always about you.
I'm finding myself babe."

I stay.

"Hold it down for me babe" I say.
"I need reassurance from you. I
have days where I feel disconnected
from you so I need you to do this for me."
you're asking for too much.

You leave.

Hold it down huh?

H a r d c o r e.
I shield my heart from the world.
I hide my emotions so deep I
forget to feel sometimes. I've built
walls as high as the great walls to
ensure no one infiltrates. I'm on
guard duty twenty-four seven to
guarantee the protection of my heart.
So, no I can't smile for you, and I can't
let myself be happy. I have to be tough.
I have to be hard. I have to be strong.
I'm hardcore because I can't be broken
again. I refuse to be broken again.

I struggle with letting go because I struggle with opening up and letting people in. The war that goes on in my mind when I attempt to let someone in is perplexing. Is this one going to be different? Are they going to stay or are they going to make me regret letting them in? Am I making the right decision? I struggle with deciding who to let in all the while wanting everyone to experience my authenticity. But I can't just let everyone experience the real me and be judged for being different or having it used against me when we're at odds. When I invest my time and energy into people and when I give them a piece of me, letting go is almost not an option. Why would I voluntarily let go of someone who I love, and I took the chance of opening myself up to? I also understand that letting go is sometimes the strongest act of love you can demonstrate. Do I lock myself away from the world to ensure my peace of minds safety? Do I hope and pray that the people I choose to open myself up to are genuine people? It's this constant battle in my head that never allows me to rest.

The struggles of opening up and letting go...

putting me through hell is all you
did and now you sit back and judge
the way i chose to manage and adapt.
destruction doesn't begin to describe
this atrocity of a scene you've created.
mood swings. insecurities. bitterness.
exhaustion. unhinged anger and violence.
no more smiling, no more peace,
no more happiness in this home, to
say the least, this is what it's come
down to. fighting every night about
the same old shit. sipping liquor in
the morning to feel sane and to
prepare for the next round of this
war you assumed you masterminded.
"what's wrong with you?"
"you've changed."
"what happened to you?"
you question in distress.
a smile forms across my face
i can't seem to contain my laugh
in such a serious situation.
'what, you don't like this version of me baby?'
'please don't look terrified now.'
'this is what you wanted, right?'
i light my blunt and survey this mass
destruction that lies in front of you and i.
'this is how you made me.'

you made me this way…

Blame me.
As you've always done
It's nothing new
for your shortcomings
for your insecurities
for your inability to love me despite my constant
feel to make excuses for you
for your lack of empathy
You've constructed me into your personal
punching bag.
I've taken jab after jab
Uppercut after uppercut
Hook after hook
It's my fault for the voice in your head telling you
that you aren't good enough.
I'm paying for your past's mistakes.
And I'll take it, I'll take it all.
But what you won't blame me for is your lack of
effort to want to heal.

I wish you would've told me to wait for you,
Instead of dragging me and leading me on,
Punishing me for loving the broken you.
I would've understood if you told me you
Just weren't ready for all that I am.
Congratulations.
You proved your point.
You weren't ready.
And now we both walk away lesser
And a more broken version of ourselves.

I would've waited.

U n l e a r n i n g.

My past wasn't too kind to me. Expressing my feelings made me annoying to be around. Asking to be reassured from time to time made me needy. Feeling proud about any accomplishments made me self-centered. Wanting my love to be reciprocated made me high maintenance. It’s not easy to act as if none of this has had negative impact on how I identify with love and relationships. I need time and patience to unlearn these habits. My past wasn’t kind. I’m hoping you’ll be kinder.

i'm envious of your pride.
the way you fight for it
like you'd die without it.
the way you'd move
mountains to ensure its
safety and protection.
the way you never budge
when it comes to anyone
or anything trying to make
you swallow it or push it to
the side. i'd do absolutely
anything and everything to
be loved by you the way
you love that pride of yours.

your pride...

Is she aware that I live rent free in your mind, that you miss me so deep you feel empty, and that sometimes you're so frustrated that you lost me; you take it out on her? What makes matters worse is that you have no one to blame but yourself. Engaging in the chase with her is the reason you risked everything for and inevitably lost me. So, you fight with your entire being forcing yourself to make it work with her because if you have to face the fact that you chose her, lost me and it failed anyways, you'd never be able to live with yourself. You have no other option but to stay because you know there's no turning back. The damage you caused is irreparable, and you know I'm not ever coming back. Is she aware that I occupy a permanent significant place in your heart and that she'll never be able to fill that void? Is she aware that you chased her, filled her head up with this fairytale dream just to settle for her?

Is she aware?

"I love you."
"I'm so sorry."
"It won't ever happen again."

You don't get tired of spewing the same old bullshit?

Like I haven't heard those words before.
Like I haven't seen that guilt before.
Like I haven't carried the burden of feeling like I must accept your apology before.

This is nothing new from you.

Your words carry no value.
Your actions have lost all meaning.
You have lost all credibility with me.

Hear me out.

I love you too.
I'm also so sorry.
It won't ever happen again because you won't get the chance to hurt me again.

Access denied.

an honorable woman would've
walked away the first time.
an honorable woman would've
ran away at the sight of the first
red flag. an honorable woman
would've ducked as you threw
the first jab at my insecurities
in attempt to make yourself feel
whole. an honorable woman
would've never allowed it to
get to this point. an honorable
woman would've stood her ground.
an honorable woman would've
guarded her honor wiser. i can't stay.
i can't hold on to hope anymore.
i'm commanding my brain to walk
away, but my heart won't follow.
my feet won't move. i'm tearing
my own heart apart. an honorable
woman's morals were compromised
all in the name of love. all because
she fell in love.

an honorable woman.

i was always worth it.
the time and energy.
the love and patience.
i was worth it all but because
i simply wasn't presented
to you on a silver platter
you ran as fast as you
could and never looked back.
you lacked vision,
but baby i was always worth it.

i was worth it...

I've constantly made it a priority
to ensure your happiness has
always been essential, my main
responsibility and majority of the time at
the expense of myself. I've paid that
price more times than I can count now.

Cheers to... H O N E S T Y.

Inadequate in quite a few areas I tried desperately to mask for you. Never appreciated the lengths I went through for you. Compassion and empathy for the person who was willing to cross oceans for you wasn't your strongest suit. Matter fact I don't believe you had a strong suit outside of being selfish. Oh, lackluster in bed was consistent for you. Just another example of me never being a priority to you in any aspect. Carrying the weight of your failures, rejections, and your insecurities because you weren't man enough to do so was exhausting. So, cheers to being honest; something you could never be.

I left footprints in the sand
hoping you'd follow through
when you were ready
instead you let the ocean
wash it all away
inconsiderate of the time
I've invested in you, in us.
All the progress, gone.
All my efforts, wasted.
What a waste you were.
There's nothing left to
savor here thanks to you.

A waste.

I was too good for you.
My kindness, my soul,
my heart. I trusted you
with the task of nourishing
my spirit. You entered like
poison slowly ridding me
of the person I prided myself
on being for so long. And,
I still would've fought for you.

You were never worthy of a woman of my caliber.

I walked into your life and immediately walked into a competition. Competing for your love and your time, but not from another woman. I was in constant competition with your pride. You struggling to decide who was worthy of being put first was the most disgraceful position you could ever put me in. The woman you love. And to know I lost that battle time and time again and stayed makes me quite disgraceful of myself.

Me vs your pride.

she's not me,
and maybe that's a good thing.
maybe she possesses what you need.
maybe despite how much I loved you,
she could love you better, she could
love you in a way you feel loved,
protected and seen.

wants vs needs.

i know you'll search for me in every
other woman you meet or come across
for every quality you took for granted
you'll pray she possess. for every time
I exhibited grace, kindness and empathy
towards you when you weren't deserving
you'll yearn for. specifically, during the
times you throw tantrums attempting to mask
your shortcomings. for the countless times I
wiped away your tears and prioritized you over
me, you'll finally understand that not everyone
is willing to put their needs to the side for
another. you'll hope they're as naïve as I was.
they'll make you suffer and pay for abusing my
love for you. you'll continuously and desperately
search hoping you won't have to come to terms
with the voices in your head telling you that you
made the gravest mistake. you'll search for me,
and you'll never find me again.

your karma...

C R U T C H.
When your ego is bruised,
When your insecurities suffocate you,
When you're in need of a boost,
You search frantically for me.
You use me.
You lean on me.
You throw all the weight on to me.
I assist in your healing.
You don't need a crutch anymore.
There's no need for me anymore.
You don't look for me anymore.
I don't want to be your crutch.

You keep saying that I fell in love with you at the wrong time. That maybe before the pain and the trauma, you could've been able to love me back. That maybe before you were broken, we could've been perfect together. But I don't believe you. And maybe that makes me wide eyed, stupid or naïve, but I don't care. I think you're scared of this. You feel yourself falling in love with me and it's scary because of all the pain you've suffered. It terrifies you so much that it makes you want to push me away or run away to avoid ruining the happiness and love you could have. I get your reasoning, but I think we're worth fighting for. I think we're worth letting both of our pasts go and giving us a clean slate. You think I fell in love with you at the wrong time, I think there's no better time than right now. You're aware of the parts of you that you're not proud of and that means you can change it, you can fix it. You can work on yourself till you become the person you feel is better equipped for us, and I'll be here every step of the way.

Love at the wrong time...

don't love me enough
to tell me you fucked up.
don't love me enough
to want to clear your
conscious of your
wrongdoings so you can
sleep peacefully at night.
don't love me enough after
you stab a knife through
my heart. love me enough
to think before you act.
love me enough to remove
yourself from situations to
avoid hurting the person you
claim to love the most. love
me enough before you hurt me.
love me enough to not stab a
knife through my heart.

love me enough.

I wish I would've known all that came with you. I wish you would've been more open about your past; I wouldn't have been so hard on you for the qualities you lacked. I wish you would've communicated more about how you felt; I wouldn't have been so cruel to you about not caring enough. I wish you would've felt more comfortable with me; there's so many issues between us that we possibly could've fixed and got over. I wish we both could've been more understanding and sympathetic towards each other; maybe we would've survived.

I wish... I wish... with all my heart.

Apparently, you were the only one who had traumas to heal from.
Apparently, you were the only one who had insecurities.
Apparently, you were the only one's past who was granted permission to play a part in the present and deserved no repercussions for it.
Apparently, you're the judge that gets to compare our pain and decide that you win the battle of who suffered worse.
You would assume that with all you suffered through; you'd be more empathetic.
I figured you would refrain from causing pain to others fully being aware of the long term affects it can have.
Instead, you became colder and crueler.

Your demons destroyed you.

Pour into me.
Nourish me.
Water me.
Prioritize me.
Protect me.
Value me.
For once,
It's all about me.
I need it to be all
About me.

me. me. me.

I've been trying to fall back in love with you
Wearing myself out trying to dismiss the pain,
Doing everything in my power to forget the
nights the pain became too unbearable,
Invalidating my feelings and the trauma I
endured in your arms just to stomach
attempting to move forward with you,
Reminiscing on the few moments we were
happy in hopes those feelings would come
rushing back and I'd find my reason to stay.
Punishing myself trying to remain in a situation
I've outgrown,
Truth is, I've exhausted every ounce of energy
I have trying to force myself to fall back in love
with you.
It's not worth it and more importantly, you're not
worth it, not anymore.
You break something enough times; it becomes
impossible to ever mend the pieces back together
again despite how much you want it to.
I guess this is what happens when you've hurt
someone to the point of no return.

to the point of no return…

I'm prepared, if this ends up being goodbye. If you finally decide I'm not what you desire anymore, if you end up exhausted of me like many have before you, if I'm more trouble than it's worth, if suddenly there's someone much more exciting than I am to you, if you wake up one day and your feelings change, I'm prepared. I've played these scenarios in my head repeatedly waiting for the other shoe to drop, waiting to prove myself right about everyone always leaving me behind. So, don't burden yourself, I promise, I'm prepared. I'm good at goodbyes. They're all I expect, they're all I know. Trust me, I've prepared for this moment right here.

Signed the overthinker...

I distance myself
From the world,
From my family,
From my friends,
From my loved one.
It's not intentional,
It's not because I don't care,
It's not because I want to isolate myself.
It's not because I don't think you wouldn't understand what goes on in my head or try to.
It's not because I don't trust you with my thoughts.
If I knew what it was, I'd scream it at the top of my lungs.
I'm praying you don't ever interpret my distance for anything other than me needing to be one with myself,
Other than me trying to understand myself,
By myself.

distance...

I know I have no grounds or rights here anymore. I know I don't get to make demands. I know that you're with her now, but you owe me. You owe me for all the pain you've caused me, all the tears I've shed over you and all the sacrifices I made that amounted to nothing in the end. You owe me! So, I'm asking you to not love her the way you loved me. I'm pleading with you to not give yourself to her the way you did me. I need to walk away with peace knowing she won't have you the I've had you. I need to know that all the hell we suffered through together won't be in vain. I need it to mean something. I need to know that despite the ugly, you saw the beauty. I need to know that although I we weren't perfect, I still hold a special place in your heart, and you won't give yourself to another the way you gave yourself to me. You owe me this much.

You owe me.

my first love,
you disappoint me.
to hold such a significant role
and fail so miserably.
you were unsuccessful at meeting expectations.
the first,
the measuring stick,
you were supposed to be one of the most
remarkable chapters in my story.
now,
you've become the saddest part of my story,
the one who robbed me of my innocence in love,
the one who's caused me to become so cold,
the one I now must tell my future daughter about
when she assumes falling in love for the first time
is going to be this magical experience.
my first love,
your disappointment runs much deeper and
further than just me.

my disappointment...

I'm tempted,
To light everything you own on fire.
To scream to the world how toxic and nauseating you are.
To get on my knees and pray the next woman is your karma.
To hope you suffer as much as you've made me suffer.
To become karma myself and ensure you pay for everything.
I see your face and the temptation grows.
Then it hits me.
The pain you've inflicted,
Is a direct reflection of you.
How I choose to react,
Reflects me.
I'm tempted,
But I wouldn't be able to stomach myself if I resorted into turning into you.
But don't tempt me...

temptations...

our little game.
screaming, fighting, and throwing dishes,
spewing every cuss word under the sun,
diminish each other as much as possible,
penalizing each other for not being perfect,
misplacing blame on both sides,
bringing past failed fights back to light in hopes
this time we'll walk away with the win,
attacking each other's character while jumping
out of character,
the sides of each other no one else is aware of.
broken glasses everywhere.
wake up the next day disgusted with our actions
and how far we allowed it to go,
we apologize, but not for how we acted,
not for the pain we've caused one another,
not for anything remotely close to the reason
everything escalated in the first place.
we apologize to avoid,
we say we're sorry, but no one takes any real
accountability.
we feel mature, like we've hit a new level of
growth.
kiss and make up.
walk hand in hand in love for the world to see.
"what a lovely couple."
they have no idea...
when we get back home,
we'll go right back to playing our game.

daddy's little girl never had a
chance because daddy created
such a mess, way early on before
she was aware that her daddy
left her on his own free will.
a daughter paying the price for
her a father's cowardly choice to
leave his flesh and blood behind.
commitment issues.
she wants to love this man and
let him in but she is struggling.
she can't love him, and she won't
let him love her all thanks to
daddy's dear old choice.
abandonment issues.
she's sacrificed herself in ways
a human being shouldn't all in
hopes to not have to watch
another man walk out of her life,
all thanks to daddy's dear old
choice. she's paying a
tremendous cost all thanks to
dear old dad who won't ever
see the magnitude of his
decision to turn his back on his
baby girl. all she wanted was to
be

daddy's little girl...

One day, you'll wake up in agony.
Regretful,
for the way you chose to devalue me.
Beating yourself up,
for not realizing sooner that although I wasn't perfect, I was still the very best part of you.
Disappointed,
in how you chose to not handle me with care I deserved.
Disgusted,
with all the woman you gave the power to look down on me because they had a piece of you the entire time I had you.
That day that it hits you,
You'll become a prisoner in your own mind,
You'll never let it go.
You'll never be able to comprehend how or why you were so selfish and ungrateful.
One day,

sorry.

Love is still here.

The love I have for you has yet to disappear. Believe me, I've tried to hate you. I've tried to erase you or turn off the love I have for you, but it's still here. My loyalty and commitment are still with you unfortunately. I despise giving you the satisfaction, but as of right now the thought of me being with another man is uncomfortable to me. I can't think of another man because it was always supposed to be you. Caring for you is embedded in my heart. I can try to hate you with my entire being, but I know if God were to come to me and tell me you've grown up, matured and changed into a better man, I'd come running back to you instantly. With tears in my eyes and this weight in my heart I still want the best for you. I hate that I love you. I hate that I weirdly still feel committed to you. I hate that I still care for you but that's what happens when you indulge in another human being. That's what happens when you've invested in another human being. The love is there, and it will always be there for you. Although I had to remove myself from you, the love is still there.

i know how this ends,
but damn i'd do anything
to just feel your heartbeat
and your skin on my skin
again. wrapped in your arms,
it was the safest i ever felt,
although i knew i was never
safe, and that says a lot about
me and my traumas. even if
i knew i'd wake up to a war
the next morning; it's not okay
but it kind of was. the world
will laugh and call me a fool
for loving you. they're right.
i know how this ends, but
i need to feel you again.

familiar ending...

you can't dictate or decide
what you went through or
what you were put through.
childhood, shitty parents,
toxic environments, and
traumatic events. but now
that you're all grown up,
you have to choose to want
better, more from yourself.
you have to decide that what
happened won't repeat itself.
not with you, not with your
children, and not with anyone
surrounding you.

deciding...

It's okay to give up sometimes. Giving up has such a negative connotation to it, but it's not always a bad thing. It doesn't mean you're weak or that you don't love someone. Sometimes you have to give up on certain things and people for your sanity. There are people who leech onto us when its beneficial for them, and they suck us dry till there's nothing left. There's absolutely nothing wrong with throwing in the towel and relinquishing the hold certain people have on you, especially when they're no good for you. If there's harm being caused to your sanity, your peace, your happiness, your mental, emotional or physical state, it's okay to throw in the towel and walk away.

Giving up...

If I could give you a break and breathe for you,
If I was able to somehow erase the pain you've suffered at the hands of people who were supposed to love and protect you,
If I could heal your wounds for you,
If there was some way to pull you out from the ocean of your traumas,
If I could carry the weight that lies on your shoulders and your heart for you,
If I could make you see what I see in you,
I would do it in a heartbeat.
I would've given everything short of my life for you to live the life you deserve.

I would save you,
If I could.

hate me if it makes you feel better.
paint me as the villain in our story
for choosing to let go of something
that's caused more harm than good
that's been slowly killing us both.
if it helps you sleep better at night.
if it makes the pain bearable for you.
if it contributes to you being able to heal.
go ahead, hate me and blame me,
tell the world it's all on me.
i'm the reason we never made it
out the other side together.
hate me if it makes letting go
and walking away easier for you.
i can take it, hate me if it helps.

hate me...

This isn't how it's supposed to be.
Contention with the bad outweighing the good.
Punishing one another for not knowing how to love the other back properly.
Beating ourselves up for feeling as if we're not good enough for the other.
Never going a day without selfishly stripping a piece away from each other trying to prove a point.
Tears and broken champagne bottles.
Glass on the floor along with our dignity.
Belittling each other in hopes that we'll feel eventually feel better about ourselves.
Screaming at the top of our lungs hoping our voice will be heard while refusing to hear the other's side.
Breaking each other down at the expense of the other.
Neither of us willing to walk away.
Neither of us willing to put our pride to the side and work on us.
Refusing to accept that this is not what love is.
This isn't how it's supposed to be.
This isn't okay.

I'm sorry... for the part I played.

I need to apologize. I wasn't perfect and I don't want to be portrayed as such. I had bad days. I contributed to the demise of us just as you did. There are so many things I wish I could go back and do differently. It might not have changed the outcome, but maybe we would've ended on better terms. Maybe we wouldn't have become something we both had to heal from. I don't want to go back. I don't want to relive the past. I just felt the need to take responsibility for the part I played. I expected you to just know how I was feeling without communicating it to you. I was never direct with what I wanted from you, and I blamed you for not figuring it out. I was childish with the way I chose to handle our relationship, and although it doesn't make the pain you caused okay. I understand now. I just... I realize now that we were two young adults trying to figure out what love was, how to love and who we were all at the same time. It was a lot to juggle. So, I'm sorry for the part I played. I apologize.

CPR

I've been applying chest compressions to this relationship on my own for some time now, CPR, pushing epi, cracking the chest, exhausting every amount of resource and drug to bring life back to this lifeless relationship. "Call it already" everyone around me who loves me and have watched me suffer for so long screams in agony. I'm panting. I'm not ready to let go yet but I don't see any other options in sight. We've been down too long.

Time of death: March 15, 2013.

I used to be strong. As time goes by, I've allowed peoples words and actions to have a much bigger impact on my life than they should. He cheated, so there must be something wrong with me. She was a bad friend, so I can't be as loving and as trusting as my heart desires. They don't agree with my life's choices so I must be doing something wrong. I've given bit and pieces of my power away to people who didn't deserve me. And now I'm not as strong or as proud of myself as I used to be. I've allowed everyone to have a say on my life. I shelter myself more, I close myself off, I'm not as open, and I work overtime trying to keep my heart out of my decision making and my life altogether. I stopped living. I stopped living for me and it led me to stop living all together. I used to be so strong and now, I've never felt weaker than I do right now.

I used to be strong...

Resentment.

I thought I'd be able to forgive you, eventually.
I'd take the time and do the work,
And one day I'd be able to look at you and see the man I fell in love with.
I figured if I took it one day at a time,
I'd be able to trust you when you tell me that you love me and won't hurt me again.
I wouldn't get extreme anxiety on an entirely new level when you're out with the guys.
I'd be able to not feel so insecure in your arms like I'm not enough for you or to keep you.
I think it just hit me that I'm not as forgiving as I thought I was.
I've worked relentlessly trying to let the past go.
I've been battling with myself for not being able to move past everything.
Like it's my fault that you lied to me, or you were unfaithful to me.
This fight, it's not a fight I want win let alone to be a part of anymore.
Attempting to force myself to forget the past and all the pain that comes along with it.
Constantly threatening myself that if I don't figure out a way to trust you again, I'm going to lose you.
When in reality, I lost you the second you gave yourself away to her.
You gave her a piece of me, in you, and that alone is unforgivable.

being young, naïve and in love
makes you turn someone who's
a liar, a cheater, and a narcissist,
unconsciously into someone who's
troubled, damaged, and broken.
you blind yourself from what's
standing right in front of you.
instead of the devil that he is,
you turn him into a distressed angel.

Chances.

I love you, I don't want to lose you, so I keep giving you chance after chance after chance.
You hurt me,
I make excuses for the pain you've caused,
You're struggling,
You're battling with something from within,
And I give you another chance.
You belittle me,
I search for a way to take the blame.
I shouldn't have angered you.
I should be less irritable.
And I give you another chance.
You lie to me,
You're just trying to protect me.
I probably would've lost it had you told me the truth upfront anyways
It's okay, I understand.
And I give you another chance.
You cheat on me,
I've let myself go,
I mean she is stunning.
I need to do more on my end, so you don't have to resort to cheating.
And I give another chance.

Chances

The more chances you give someone to hurt you, the higher the chances are that they're going to hurt you again.

There are somethings that don't deserve a second chance. There are somethings people must take accountability for. There are somethings people need to face repercussions for and sometimes the repercussion needs to be losing you permanently.

Love is not a good enough excuse to stay especially when everything is at stake.

Never allow someone to get comfortable with hurting you.
They'll never stop once they know you'll never walk away.

I Won't Apologize For What I'm About To Say…

Say when,
When it becomes too much for your soul to bare.
When it becomes something that requires far
more than you can provide.
When it takes away from you being true to
yourself.
When you know it's time but you're afraid of
what's on the other side.
Say when,
And deal with the fallout afterwards.
Know when to say when...

Why didn't you fight for me?

I have absolutely no business writing you right now, but I can't rest. I need to know why. Why didn't you fight for me when I left? I was your everything and you never wanted to experience life without me, those were your words. You said I was your princess and you loved me. So please explain how you could say that to me and when I left, you didn't fight for me. You didn't buy flowers. You didn't blow my phone up trying to reconcile. There were no apologies on your end. You didn't even attempt to get in touch with me to just see how I was doing. How does one tell you that you're their entire world and not put up a fight to keep you? You treated me like I was so easily disposable to you, and I just can't wrap my head around that. So, I need to know... I need to know why.

boys they're disposable.
friends are replaceable.
they'll come and they'll go,
but when you meet that person
who becomes your person,
who completes you in a way,
no other human being could ever
like our souls met in another lifetime.
it was destiny for us to meet again.
you never imagine life without them.
i never thought it would happen to us.
inseparable. intune. indescribable.
the bond we formed,
the promises and secrets,
the inside jokes no one will ever understand.
i imagined it would take death
to separate you and i
and now you're gone.
a piece of me is gone.
heartbreaks are whatever,
you heal and you move on.
friendships end,
it hurts, but you move on.
but how on earth,
do you move on
from your person?

i lost my best friend.

You'll never really know me. You gave birth to me, and you raised me. You think that means you know me better than anyone in this world could, but you don't. Instead of creating a space for me to unapologetically be me, you placed all your traumas, your disappointments, your shortcomings, and your expectations on to me. Just to call me a failure for not living up to who you wish you would've been when you had the chance to be someone. Having shoes created for you to step into when it's not who you want to be, has created this rift between us. You don't know me, and it's heartbreaking that you don't try to get to know me. I'm not who you envisioned I'd be, and you've punished me for it since I can remember. Now whoever goes first, between you and I, whoever dies first; we'll both know that you never really knew me.

family ties...

I'm always overreacting,
when I arrive to confront disrespect.
I'm always overreacting,
when I don't turn a blind eye to being used.
I'm always overreacting,
when I refuse to bite my tongue.
I'm always overreacting,
when I demand in return what I provide.
I'm always overreacting,
when I'm not allowing bullshit.

I'll continue overreact to get what I deserve...

Resentment
Anger
Fear
Roads that lead nowhere
Except to your own demise
Along with the demise of hope, happiness and peace.

haven.
when chaos overrides peace
you contribute this sense of relief.
hesitation has never occurred
when my imperfections get the best of me.
you refrain from holding me back
allowing me to shine at my brightest.
my being broken has never struck fear
in you or the way you choose to love me.
it's the composure and patience that you display.
when my past or my traumas play out.
it's something I never take for granted
the sanctuary that your spirit provides.

She's like a deer
Hard to read
Easily spooked
At the sign of change.
Patience and moving at ease
Are requirements to get close.
Constant reassurance
that you're here
For the long run
For the right reasons.
You can't force anything
You can't move too fast
Her instincts are to run.
She's been programmed
To never allow anyone
to get too close to her.

was she everything you dreamed of?
did she spark a fire in you that I never could?
did she celebrate your wins harder than I did?
was she more comforting through the bad?
she couldn't have been that amazing,
because here you are back at my feet
begging for forgiveness and to fix things
you mean to tell me you risked everything
for nothing, nothing at all?

a failed risk...

Being loved by you created an environment where I could flourish. I was not only encouraged to thrive, but to shine as bright as I could. It's like I'm a light bulb that was never properly taken care of prior to you. Someone walked outside and realized they needed light to see in the dark. They got the light bulb, screwed the light bulb in, but they didn't secure it. They didn't ensure that it was stable and prepared to withstand anything that came its way. They didn't handle it with the care that it required so there were times where the light bulb would flicker or even dim. Sometimes it would even shut off. But you were different. You provided this gentle touch I've been seeking for so long. You screwed the light bulb into place. You stepped back and admired in amazement afterwards. You made it okay for me to shine and to never apologize for it. Being loved by you made me want to love myself more. It made me better.

Being loved by you...

P R E S S U R E.
I'm feeling an immense amount of pressure
From all angles pulling me from side to side
Telling me to be someone or to be something
That I didn't ask to be or made an agreement to be.
To live up to a version of me that never existed
or
a version of me that they've created in their minds.
S T O P.

I dreamed of receiving closure from you. I truly felt I deserved it. I believed with all the hell you put me through it was the least you could do for me. It was the least you owed me. Now some will say they need closure to be able to move on, but that's not the case for me. I can admit it. Deep down I wanted closure for my ego. I wanted you to come to me and own up to your mistakes; take accountability for torment you inflicted on me all these years. Say it out loud and beg for my forgiveness so I could tell you that you don't have it nor deserve it. I needed a way to hurt you back. I wanted you to come to me on your knees pleading with me not to hold the past against you, so I didn't walk away feeling so useless. I spent years building up your ego. All the jabs I took for you to feel more powerful or dominant, it was the least you could do. I wanted to be the one to tell you no, to make you feel guilty, and to cause a little pain to you on my end.

I need to be your karma.

I deserve to be loved out loud.
Honestly. Unapologetically. Purely.
I deserve to be loved out loud.
Honored for the world to hear.
Proud for the world to see.

“I love you.”
It should outweigh everything.
So why is the disrespect so deafening?
Why are the lies so heavy on my heart?
Why can’t I look past the deceit?
Love is everything.
Hearing I love you is everything.
Except when you abuse and devalue it enough it simply just becomes three meaningless words.

Meaningless words.

Being loved by me is an honor.
To be loved by someone who allows room for growth.
Who never expects perfection,
Who understands that everything in life isn't simply black or white, good or bad,
Who'll engage in war over their loved ones,
Who allows you the freedom to be you,
Who never sets limits on you or how far you can go,
Who encourages you to live in your truth,
Who gives you the room to dream as big as you can,
Who's not afraid of the imperfect sides of love,
Who holds you accountable,
Who doesn't place restrictions on how bright you should shine,
Being loved by me is a gift that should cherished.

Loved by me...

To my daughter...

Oh, for I have suffered at the hands of a man for so long. I handed him my power on a silver platter and allowed him to dictate everything. I gave him the rights to me, my feelings and my heart. He took advantage of me and as much I loathe myself for it, I hope I suffered enough for the both of us. I hope you're much stronger than I ever was. I hope from the early stages of your life you understand the value of living your life on your terms. I pray you never underestimate your power. I'd give anything for you to never sit around and let another human being decide your life for you. I'll do my absolute best by you but ultimately, it's up to you. I don't want you to be anything like I was. Yes, indeed I am much stronger now, but I hope it doesn't require you having to suffer the way I did to reach that level of strength. Please shine your light so bright it stuns and then eliminates everything sent to poison your soul. Me suffering is one thing, but the thought of you possibly suffering is unbearable. Shine bright my baby, shine your light.

My heart...
I placed my most prized possession,
my most valuable asset,
in the palm of your hands,
and you swore with your being,
you'd protect and fight for it,
as if it would kill you if you didn't.
not only did you mishandle it,
but you broke it into a million pieces.
and refused to acknowledge what you did.
you broke it and you blamed me
for the destruction your hands caused.

I always figured with time; we'd find our way back to each other. We'd take the time needed and we'd experience growth. We'd experience love elsewhere and we'd learn from them how to love better. I figured we'd become more aware of all that love entails. I had hopes we'd be more mature, and we'd be better equipped for each other. I always figured we'd find our way back to each other, but now I see there's a reason we drifted away from each other in the first place. We didn't separate to eventually find our way back to one another. We separated because we're no good for each other. We we're supposed to use our relationship as what not to do if you want to make it work. Our relationship was supposed to serve as a reminder that some things are irreparable. You and I, we were never meant to make it out together.

Irreparable…

I have no interest in being chosen anymore
By anyone or anything. I don't need the
Validation I used to seek from the world.
Choose me, pick me, want me, need me,
Or else I hold no value to myself or anyone.
I used to allow my worth to orbit around
What I assumed others would want from me
What I figured others would need from me,
Who I was told I needed to be,
The amount of despair and suffering
That surrounded my life trying to live up
To the expectations of the world nearly killed me.
I have no interest in being chosen anymore,
It's done me more harm than it ever did good.
I've accepted me for me, and I've chosen me.
The level of peace that settled in with that choice,
Let's just say, I'll never burden myself seeking
The approval of the world ever again.

No interest in being chosen...

Are we even now?

I hurt you and you've been punishing me forever for it. I made a mistake that you seem in no rush to stop reminding me of every chance you get. You won't let me live it down, and you won't allow us to move forward from it. We've been sitting in the same place I made that mistake, and we haven't moved since. I've put in the work. I've lied in the bed I made with no hesitation or rebuttal. I didn't fight it and I've given you time. I've let so much slide, because I know I did this. I'm aware that I can't dictate how you should react or how long this reaction should last because I'm the cause of it. But at what point does "healing" become torturing and trying to get even?

There's a reason you're in so much pain. There's a reason you're devastated, and you feel like you can't breathe just thinking about it. Yes, obviously you're going through a heartbreak, but there's another factor to it. There was once something there that made you so happy that you couldn't imagine life with it. There was something there that contributed so much joy and laughter to your life. There were moments, memories, milestones, and so much more that factor into this. The reason it hurts so bad is because at one point it felt so good. So, hold on to that. The reason heartbreaks hurt so much more is because there were times where it felt too good to be true, and we shouldn't forget it, or lessen that because it didn't work out.

The other side of heartbreak...

You have to give people room,
Room to not be perfect
Room to make mistakes
Room to try new things and not be belittled for it not working or it being more difficult than it was presented.
Room to be human.
Room to have dreams outside of your expectations.
Room to grow.

I'll admit it once you've been stuck in a toxic relationship for so long there are traits that latch on to you so much that they become your new normal. So, I'm not used to calm. I'm not used to reasoning and understanding. I'm not used to compromising or coming to a middle ground. I'm not used to communicating properly. This is all new to me. I'm used to screaming and cursing to get my point across. I'm used to shutting down or running away when things get hard. I'm used to this toxic way of life. I'm not proud or accepting of it. I'm just hoping for some patience and compassion as I work on reevaluating myself. And if it's not something you think you can be a part of, I won't hold you to it. There's won't be any grudges or hard feelings on my end. I get it, I have to work on healing and checking myself on the parts of me I'm not proud of.

Check myself...

i'm a train wreck.
a lost cause
currently struggling
to cope with the pain.
it's eating me alive.
i think it's winning.

P H Y S I C A L T O U C H.

Welcome to my love language.
Physical touch.
It's not just about the sex.
It's not just about the kissing.
It's feeling your warmth.
It's hearing your heartbeat
And sometimes hearing it in sync with mine.
It's also listening to your breathing.
It's touching the hairs on your body.
It's running my fingers on your skin.
It's you holding my face when you kiss me.
It's embracing your touch.
It's wrapping your arms around my waist
And me feeling invincible in your arms.
It's holding my hands and me feeling as if
the world couldn't stand a chance against us.
It's you laying on me or me laying on you,
And feeling like our souls are intertwining.
It's watching your eyes staring at me,
And me getting nervous after all this time.
Your physical touch is everything to me.
Your physical touch is everything for me.

i ignored the red flag purposely.
i didn't want to risk losing you
over something that seemed so
minuscule at the time being.
i didn't want to miss out on a
chance at real love, something
i'd been longing for so long.
i didn't want it to ever feel like
i was judging anyone's past or
their life circumstances.
i ignored the red flag purposely
just to continuously watch it
cause so many issues throughout
the entirety of our relationship.
but relationships aren't supposed
to be easy right so i fought harder
to ignore it and act as if it was okay.
i ignored the red flag purposely
just for it to eventually lead to
the demise of you and i.
all the time i wasted trying to
ignore it and hoping it would
go away with time.
all the energy i exhausted.
i ignored the red flag purposely,
and i paid the price for it every day.

ignoring the red flag...

"too much"

I was always "too much" for you.
I was "too" independent for you
So, I changed
then I became "too" reliant on you.
I was "too" confident for you
So, I changed
then I became "too" insecure for you.
I was "too" in love with you
So, I changed
then I became "too" focused on everything
outside of you.
Ultimately,
After changing myself and my life
In order to please you I realized
Nothing I ever do or did for you
Was ever going to be enough for you
Because you never loved me,
In fact, I'm betting you never liked me.
You just saw me as someone you could
Use to feel better or break to feel better.
Either way, at the end of the day.
I was always "too much" for you.
In terms of I was always too good for you.

The father shaped hole in my heart...
I want to trust him so badly. I want to give him my heart, but I can't. I can't let my guard down because I'm terrified all the time. I can't breathe because I'm scared that he won't be any different than you were to me. I'm always expecting him to leave. I keep preparing my mind for that moment to arrive. How the do you plan a future like that? How do you have any peace living like that? How the hell do I give this man my heart and hope he doesn't break it when the first man that ever loved me left and never looked back? He won't ever get the whole version of me because you broke me. My own father mishandled my heart. How am I supposed to believe this stranger is going to be different when you couldn't be? Now trust issues have been ingrained in me the second you turned your back on me. I run at the sight of commitment. I probably won't ever allow a man to love me completely. My heart won't ever be whole with the father shaped hole in my heart.

can i take you home
to forget the world,
lose myself in you,
maybe mask our pain
for a few and hope
we're both mature
enough to forget it
happened tomorrow
and not hold it
against each other?

I used to believe in my soul, in my gut, that we kept finding our way back to each other because we were soulmates. We were destined to be together, and no amount of time or temporary people would stop the inevitable. You and I were end game. I figured our love was being tested through every obstacle and relationship we encountered outside of one another. And if we fought for each other, we'd get that happily ever love. I'm starting to realize that it wasn't our love that was being tested, it was my growth. Am I strong enough to walk away and stay away from the person I love who's proven time and time again they're no good for me? Or do I allow myself to keep getting sucked back into the same old cycle? We're not soulmates. We're not this fairytale love story. You're the test I'm going to keep repeating till I pass.

The growth test.

i don't want your love.
the love you have to
enlist the aid of wars for.
the love i have to
earn for. the love i
have to keep proving
myself for. the love
you have to look down
on me for. the love i
have to compete for
i don't want love that's
filled with fear, anger and pain.
and you've confirmed that's
the only love you can provide.
so please, don't love me.
i don't want to be loved by you.
your love costs too much,
and the return isn't worth it.

Costly love...

I never imagined I could be loved.
I mean to be loved when you feel so
Broken, unfixable and unlovable
Is all I ever hoped for from someone.
It was my dream for someone to
See past all the flaws and all the
Damage. To give me the
Opportunity to not be defined
By the unfortunate cards I was dealt.

To be loved...

I can't let the history repeat itself. Broken homes, absentee parents, leaches as friends and family, the bare minimum requirements. I want to create new standards and healthy habits for everyone surrounding me, but most importantly for the seeds I bare on this earth. My children, my children's children and their children. The ones I leave behind far after I'm gone. I want better for them. I can't leave this earth knowing that they'll suffer the way I once did with parents berating each other inside a broken home. Parents walking in and out at their own convenience. Friends and family sucking you dry and calling you disrespectful or messy for standing up for yourself or saying no more. I want healthy boundaries in place. I want actively healing or healed souls. I want peace and happiness as main priorities. I've suffered enough for the rest of my bloodline. I can't allow history to replay now or after I'm gone. I'm breaking generations of trauma and pain and curses. It ends with me.

Breaking generational trauma...

Make it easy for me.
Rip the bandaid off.
Walk away from me.
Tell me you don't love me.
Do whatever it takes.
Say whatever it takes.
Because if it's on me,
If it has to be my decision
To walk away from you.
I'll never follow through.

MISTAKES

A necessary part of life that not everyone is going to appreciate or understand; rightfully so if you're on the other end having to pick up all the pieces. Mistakes create opportunity for growth. It reminds us that we're all human. Now there are mistakes that follow you for the rest of your life. Some you just can't fix, but you can learn from it. It shouldn't be held against you forever, but you also must accept the repercussions some mistakes come with. Don't punish yourself for something you've been given another day of life to learn from and change.

You were competing with me.
I was rooting for you to win.
You were envious of me.
I was cheering the loudest for you.
You were struggling to congratulate me.
I was praying for you to find your path, your way.
You had so much hatred in your heart for me.
I would've taken a bullet because I loved you so much.
Your mind told you that very win of mine was a loss for you.
My mind was programmed to believe every win of mine was an opportunity for both of us to shine.
See the difference between you and I,
I loved you and your happiness was a priority to me.
You despised me because your ego and pride were always your main priority.

The difference between you and me.

I don't want to be strong anymore. It's exhausting. Repeatedly having the weight of the world on your shoulders and no one thinks twice of it because "you're strong." If being strong means I have to always face everything alone and be expected to find a way to get through, I don't want it. If being strong means not only do I have to carry my burdens but the burdens of everyone else as well, I don't want it anymore. If being strong means everyone assumes I have it under control at all times and I'm not allowed to not be okay or need help some days, I don't want it anymore. I need help. I need to not be okay sometimes and it be completely okay. I need to be checked on. I need to not feel like it's always me against the world. I can't be strong anymore if it means it's on me and only me, every single time. I physically, mentally and emotionally can't be the strong anymore.

"You're so strong."

the woman i am today,
would put the woman
i once was to shame.
although it took every
ounce of the woman i
was to become this
unstoppable force i
am today. i know she'd
be proud of the growth
and the evolution. she'd
be okay with being put
to shame rather than
years going by and still
being the same woman.

a new woman.

I don't need you to be my everything
It's impossible to be my everything
You could never be my everything
All I ask is that in the process of loving me,
you allow me to be me.

its stressful, putting the needs and wants of everyone around you before the needs and wants of yourself. pacing around trying to make sure everyone's okay while you're confused and at war with yourself. losing bits and pieces of you every time you tell yourself that your wants and needs arent important at the moment. not prioritizing yourself means you're not really living. and when you're not really living, you're the saddest version of yourself.

you deserve better.

I'm in this repetitive cycle
where I need time to myself.
where I know if don't take
that time to reenergize, to
refocus, and to be one with
myself, the chain reaction
that'll follow will be
catastrophic to the work I've
put in from within. but I'm
also aware of how it may
come off to the people I love
the most. I never want them to
feel as if they don't matter to
me or that I take their kindness
and love for granted. I hope
they don't take it personal
and they understand that it
has absolutely nothing to do
with them, and everything to
do with me.

me time.

guilt can be exhausting
and it stunts growth.
it imprisons you.
it keeps you from living
your truest form.
guilt from wanting more,
guilt from walking away,
guilt from choosing you,
guilt from not wanting to settle,
guilt from making mistakes you can't go back in time and fix.
guilt is a bitch.
and it'll kill you,
if you don't take accountability,
forgive,
and let go.

guilty as charged.

i do miss you sometimes,
mostly
when i'm horny
or when i'm lonely.
other than that,
there's nothing to miss.

when it becomes painful
to walk away and to stay
pick the poison that won't
cause long lasting effects.

I walked away because I was aware I had too much baggage to carry, too many demons to fight and I'd admit it, I was in no hurry to change or heal. I've exhausted so much energy fighting wars that cost me more than you could ever imagine. I wouldn't have been able to love you the way you deserved. I'm not ready to heal, put the work in and forgive. Mentally, I'm not there yet. I need a break from fighting. Fighting the world, fighting myself, and fighting people who were supposed to love me. With that being said, I knew me struggling was going to do more harm than good to you. I couldn't live with myself knowing I caused damage to someone who just wanted to love me. I'm sorry I couldn't be what you needed or deserved from me. I'd rather apologize for walking away and hurting you now than to apologize years later for the trauma I caused you that you can't recover from.

I'm sorry...

Feelings.
Intense.
I feel everything to the core.
From the smallest, simplest things,
To the large, meaningful things.
My heart feels so deep.
I'm not overexaggerating.
I'm not overreacting.
Everything I feel is real and it's loud.
Deafening.
There is no ignoring,
There is no telling myself it's not that deep
When my heart is screaming otherwise.

you ruined the idea of love for me.
i'll admit, i might've had some
very unrealistic expectations of
what i assumed love would be
and how I imagined it'd feel.
but to turn love into something
i feel the need to avoid, to turn
it to something i'm terrified of.
it's unforgivable.

love sucks

downplaying the love we shared huh?
the tears you shed on my chest,
the times I laid all your doubts to
rest so you could believe in you,
the safe place I provided for you
where you'd disclose all your
fears and burdens to without
any judgement being passed around.
the repeated reassurance and
words of affirmation I made sure
to give you on days I needed it for myself most.
you can try to downplay us all you
want, but you know the significant
role I played in your life.
you and I both know.

my role.

I attempted everything under the sun, but it remained crystal clear that you would never be able to love me the way that I've loved you. You'd never be able to prioritize me the way that I've prioritized you. You'd never be able to sacrifice for me the way I've done for you time and time again. I loved you the way I breathed, naturally. It wasn't forced and I never questioned it. It was like something I'd been doing my entire life but loving me wasn't the same for you. It was a chore for you, something you got stuck having to do. Something you despised having to do, but you sucked it up. Frustrated and annoyed you did it simply out of obligation. You struggled tremendously and I think that's what hurt the most. For me, loving you was so easy and for you, loving me was this constant hassle.

I tried to love you...

watch the way you talk to me,
i'm not the weak-willed woman
i once was. i've grown so much
since then, and when i tell you
the things i once allowed won't
be tolerated anymore by anyone,
i simply mean watch the way you talk to me.

I'm afraid the only peace
we'll ever find with one
another is the day we
say goodbye to each other.

thank you for not giving
up on me. I know because
of him I've displayed some
questionable moments and
qualities, probably created
doubts to you about where
my morals and values lied,
but thank you for loving me
anyways. thank you for never
holding it against me. thank you
for continuously wiping my tears
away and building me back up.
thank you for always being an
ear for me to talk to and never
judging me in the process. I
don't take it lightly, the grace
and patience you've exhibited.

my friend...

<u>obligation.</u>
"she's my wife."
"we have kids."
"we live together."
"I have to stay and make it work."

I never want anyone to feel obligated to stay with me or to make it work with me. I don't deserve to be just tolerated. I'm a force to be reckoned with. I'm a selfless, honorable and fierce woman. I deserve to be loved. I deserve to have someone who wants to love me. Someone who admires my heart and wants to stand firmly by my side – honored and proud to love me and to be loved by me. It's a slap to the face to reside by my side out of obligation and not love.

<u>love.</u>
"I'm in love with her."
"I don't want a life without her in it."
"loving her is what I want to do for the rest of my life."
"losing her is losing myself and that's not an option.

i'm not interested in loving
in survival mode anymore.
living my life as if i'm in combat,
fighting a war, feeling as if my back is
always against the wall, never getting to
sit down and breathe. never having space
to enjoy being loved, cared and nurtured
because my guard is up all the time.
constantly living in fear it's draining
me. no more looking over my
shoulders, never feeling free.
i want comfort. i want peace
and i want to love freely and feel again...

survival mode.

I don't want to tie you down.
If I'm the shackles that keep
you from being free, let me
know and I'll let you be.
I never want to cage that heart of yours,
Even if I do want you all to myself.

When things get hard, I run as fast as I can. I run because I'm afraid to see the destruction when things aren't okay. I'm terrified of dealing with the aftermath of it all. It triggers my mind into thinking the end is near and my first instinct is to run. I run to keep the happy moments and memories as my last reminder of us - rather than to stay, watch everything fall apart and the worst sides of us become the memory that not only sticks, but overrules all the good. I'm not proud of it. I wish I wasn't like this, but I'm a runner.

I'm a runner...

drifting away...
i feel you slipping away from me
and there's nothing i can do to stop
it. you don't love me anymore and
you're trying your best not to hurt
me, so you stay. you do everything
in your power to fight off the feeling.
you think you're sparring me the pain
and the heartache. when in reality,
you're only contributing to it because
you assume I'm stupid and I don't feel
you pulling away from me. I can feel
your energy and it's causing doubt in me
about me, let's be honest, we're not
going to last and this is ending.
it's time we both come to terms
with that before we hate each other.
i can't have you hating me for you
falling out of love with me and not
being able to express that only leads
to you building resentment towards me.
i don't want to hate you for falling out
of love me. you've been gone a long
time ago. emotionally and mentally
you haven't been here in a while.
so, I've prepared for this moment.
I knew it was coming eventually.
and now it's here.

I don't want the best for you,
If it's to benefit you and her.
For you to be happy with her.
I just can't... not now.
I'm not that mature,
And I'm not that over you.

Walls.

I've built these walls.
Tall and sturdy.
To ensure no one makes it over.
Not because I don't want to be loved.
Not because I want to be alone.
Not because I want to suffer.
But simply because,
I concluded that if I let someone in, loved them and gave them everything in me,
And it didn't work out or it all fell apart,
I wouldn't make it.
I know I wouldn't be able to survive that kind of pain,
Not again.

I'm not sure we're
making it out
together hand in
hand, but I'm sure
as hell going to
enjoy the ride
till the wheels
fall off and it's
over. Somethings
weren't meant to
last, somethings
you just enjoy for
the time being.

my door.
it stays open.
i make sure to keep it wide open.
hoping you don't ever feel unwelcomed or unwanted.
anticipating your return one day
that you'll come back to me
or you'll come back for me.
like how sometimes people forget their keys or their wallet.
unaware and unintentionally sometimes you forget the most important things.
i'm trusting that you'll come back.
expecting.
hoping.
wishing.
either way,
my door is open.

boyfriend.
girlfriend.
wife.
husband.
brother.
sister.
cousin.
aunt.
uncle.

find who you are outside
of those titles. find your
own identity.

outside of myself,
you're the best part of me.
you're the best thing that
ever happened to me.

I told you I was afraid to love.
I was afraid to open my heart
up again because of my past,
but here I am wanting you
more and more every day.
So, I'm choosing to say
fuck fear, fuck what may
or may not happen in the
future. I'm choosing right
now and I'm choosing now
with you by my side.
I'm choosing to love. I'm
choosing to follow my heart
and it leads me right to you.
I'll do the work; I'll play my role.
I want us to have a real chance
and you're worth every fear I have
of what could possibly go wrong.
I choose you, every single time.

I choose you.

You told me not to fight for you,
You told me I deserved better than you,
You told me there'd be nothing to gain,
And that I'd lose loving you.
I hate I didn't listen to you.

You were right.

It's not easy to not change.
To see how the world doesn't appreciate someone that loves loud and very hard,
And not change.
To see how many times one's kindness can get taken for weakness,
And not change.
To see how intimidating and insecure you being confident makes some people,
And not change.
To see how people with big hearts continuously get treated so disposably,
And not change.
Trust me,
I'm not weak for not changing myself.
If anything, I'm stronger for not allowing the world or past experiences to dictate how I love, how I treat myself and others.

I can't change...

we were both broken
around the same time
and maybe that's why
we were drawn towards
each other, for both of
us to see the beauty in
a broken soul and translate
that message to ourselves.

dear diary,
I hate that I'm in a place in my life where I'm expecting to be hurt, expecting people not to show up for me, expecting to be disappointed and expecting people to let me down. I've gone through this so many times and unintentionally, mentally and emotionally, I'm prepared for it. I hate that my mind has normalized pain. I get that it's a part of life but to be in a mindset where you anticipate ache or misery, it's not a way to live. A heart can only take some much before it becomes beyond repair. I truly feel like I'm beyond repair at this point.

You used to be my comfort zone,
Now you've become the war zone.
You've become someone I try to avoid.
You've become someone I need to escape.
You've become someone I need protection from.

she was magic.
the way she stopped
an entire room when
she'd walk in.
the way she pulled
greatness out of
anyone she'd come
in contact with.
the way her smile
and her laugh could
change your entire
mood.
the way people who've
known her forever
talks about her like
she's God like.
the way you gravitate
towards her no matter
how hard you try not to.
the way she never
identified herself as
better than anyone.
she was different.
and she never had to
tell anyone how different
she was.
you just watched her and
you could see it, sense it.
she was pure, beautiful, magic.

he says he doesn't care.
he tells everyone they
can go to hell. he says
he's fine. everyone
accepts it and walks away.
better to just accept it
than to stick around and
find out there's more to
him than what meets the
eye. everyone gives up so
soon. leading him to believe
he's not worth the trouble.
he's not worth fighting to
get to know better and to
love. he doesn't know that I
see. that cold, dark front he
puts up is because he does
care. his heart has been ripped
apart far too many times to
give anyone the right to hold
it again. mommy and daddy
didn't protect him the way they
were supposed to and now
he must deal with all the
fallout. can't trust. won't love.
hearts closed off. feelings
tucked so far, they're out of
reach.
And still, I see him.
I see through it all.

<u>forgive and forget</u>

you want me to forgive
and forget everything.
to convince my mind
that I somehow
exaggerated the pain
I suffered at your hands.
I shed oceans of tears
for the hell of it.
I broke my own heart not
believing your lies.
I made myself insecure for
your inability to be faithful.
you want me to rebuild the
trust that you broke.
I see, you're not interested in
taking any accountability here.
us falling apart is on me so it's
on me to fix everything.
you want me to forgive you,
and right now, I'd much
rather just forget you.
forget the supposed love
we've shared over the years.
forget anything and everything
that has to do with you and i.
you're not worth remembering.

Someday,
You'll fall in love again.
It won't be intentional.
You've built these walls up
And you have guards standing
At attention for one job only,
To protect that heart of yours.
But one day,
You won't have a choice in the matter.
Unintentionally,
You'll meet this person that
Gives you this magnetic pull
Where you can't stay away.
Where the fear of getting your
Heartbroken becomes irrelevant.
You'll fall in love again,
And you'll hate yourself
Forever thinking that this feeling
Wasn't worth getting back out there
And trying again for it.

who are you to ruin
the love I found outside
of you when you were
incapable of contributing
anything positive to my life?

you don't have to suffer anymore. you can put the bottles of liquor and the pill bottles down. you don't have to stop yourself from feeling. you can stop running. you can heal. you can choose to live different, to love different, and to be different. your past isn't you. surrender to the feeling that makes you believe you can't be happy; you can't be at peace or that you can't be loved. it's not going to be easy, but it's not impossible. the life you desire, it's not impossible to reach or to live it. you just have to fight for it. fight for that life that you want the way someone should've fought for you when you needed it.

you have to fight.

"If you loved me, why'd you leave me?"

The real question should be if you loved me, how could you not see how miserable I had gotten over time? How could you not see how broken I've been? How could you not feel how distant I had become? How could you not realize the affects your actions were having on me? I was right in front of your face shattered in pieces on the floor like a broken mirror after a fist has been put through. The simple fact that I was suffering being with you and it never appeared to you says more than you could ever imagine. Don't ever question my love for you because while I was in anguish, I still tried to love you. So much that you never noticed I was slowly dying on the inside. If you loved me, why'd you break me?

I can't defend our love anymore. I can't look in the eyes of the people I love and explain to them why I love you. I can't explain to them why I'm fighting so hard to make it work with you. How do I defend the love we share when I'm questioning why the hell I'm still here with you? Our connection is severed. I can't find the words to justify why I'm still here. I can't pretend any longer that this is okay – that this is how love is supposed to be. If I can't advocate for us, there should be no us.

It's over.

I'm not here to be controlled.
to be told what to do or how
to do it or how to be or how
to act. I'm no one's puppet.
I march the beat of my own
drum, securely and proudly.
I live for me, and I make the
decisions for me. no one
gets to walk into my life
dictate anything. You don't
control the things and the
people you love. you're
supposed to enjoy them
for whom they are. Sit back
and experience being loved
by them. But control? That's
not love and that's no way to
love.

you don't control me...

trusting you without any
proof or actively seeing
you attempting to better
yourself was my greatest
mistake to this day.

I know the love
we share is real
because I need a
break from the
world and all I
want is to be with
you.

you made a habit
out of hurting me
and calling it love.
disgraceful.

I haven't been the same since you and I ended things. Before you start letting your mind wonder, it's not because I miss you or I want you back. I do think I miss the idea of you though. Who I thought you'd be for me when we got together, I miss that. But most importantly, I think underestimated this whole breaking up process. I didn't realize how much I'd have to readjust my life. I didn't realize how much of a role you played in my life till you were gone. Now I have mornings when I wake up, grab my phone expecting a good morning text from you and I'll admit, I get disappointed. Or when something funny happens and I reach for my phone to text or call you, and it hits me that I can't do that anymore. or when I'm watching a movie and I see the empty space beside me where you use to lay, I get sad. Or nights when I'd get ready for bed, you'd lay down behind me and wrap your arms around me like you needed me to fall asleep, it makes me want to cry. The routine we shared throughout our relationship makes this whole process almost unbearable. It painful having to deal with all these changes.

Changes...

selfishly,
i want to keep
you all to myself.
indulge in and love you.
but the world deserves
to experience your fire,
your passion and your light.
i'd be wrong to keep
you away from the world.

there's no forgetting the pain, history or memories. there's no erasing or going back and changing what has already happened. but there is healing. there's not allowing what's happened to take power over you. there's not allowing it to trigger you into a version of yourself that you're not proud of. there's taking your life back into your hands and living on your own terms.

I'm selfish, and I'm not going to sit here and be apologetic about it or tell you that I want to change because I don't. I don't have an issue with being selfish. You didn't see the carnage that being completely selfless bought me. I was broken, drained and I wasn't anywhere near myself. I gave and gave, and I got nothing in return. You don't know what that does to a person. Feeling like giving your everything wasn't enough and now you're left with nothing and nobody. So, I've learned that being selfish to an extent with yourself isn't a bad thing. I get to walk away from relationships and situations that aren't working out intact, whole. I leave and I'm still me because I didn't sacrifice myself or compromise myself for anyone.

I'll be selfish...

I wish I could shut the voices in my head telling me I'm not enough, that I'm letting everyone around me down, that I'm a disappointment. It'd be nice to feel sane for a second.

2.a.m.
I miss you so much. I hate feeling bad or feeling like I'm disrespecting myself by missing you. we shared too much of our lives together for me to act as if it didn't happen because we ended, and you weren't perfect. yes, we're not together anymore, but those memories don't disappear. I can miss you and not go back to you. I can miss parts of you while recognizing there were bad parts of you that weren't kind to me or my heart. so, tonight I miss you like crazy. I miss your warmth. I miss hearing your laugh at my stupid jokes. I miss every part of you, the good and the bad because either way I still had you. I miss you. I want to say it out loud without looking like a basket case or without people thinking I'm going back to you. there's nothing wrong with missing you and the more I try to run from that feeling, the more I miss you and want to go back to you. instead of acknowledging my truth. I miss the hell out of you sometimes so much that I feel like I'm suffocating.

i don't want to force
myself to be okay
or comfortable with
something that is
disruptive to my spirit.

you were the silver lining.
positive. hopeful. consoling.
you made the days where
life seemed useless and
not worth living, worth
waking up and trying.
you made nights where I'd
usually cry myself to sleep,
into nights I didn't want to
sleep because for the first
time, living felt better than
dreaming.
you made moments I'd normally
put my head down and hide in
my little shell terrified of the
world into moments I stood in
my truth confidently.
for every time I seen a storm
coming towards me, I'd see the
sun prepared to shine afterwards.
all because of you.

to be loved.
to be happy.
to be respected.
to be treated with kindness.
It's not too much to ask for.
It's not to be begged for.

it's something about night,
something about darkness
that heightens all these
feelings i've tried to bury
all day. sadness, loneliness,
missing people i shouldn't,
blaming myself for things
beyond my control. thinking
'why would anyone love me?'
or feeling like i'm never
enough when i'm reliving
painful memories over and
over again. death and thoughts
of "would anyone miss me?"
racing through my mind. i
can't sleep. It's something
about the night that does
this to me.

when 12 o clock midnight strikes.

I don't fault you for
not being perfect, I
blame you for not
caring enough about
me or yourself to
take the steps to
prevent hurting
me from the things
you did have complete
control over. that,
I do fault you for.

I imagine all the time who I could be if my past didn't happen to me, if my insecurities didn't overshadow me, if my childhood wasn't so toxic and traumatic, if I didn't lose some of the most important people to me when I needed them the most, if someone would've fought for me when I couldn't have fought for me. I imagine all the time what my life could've been.

What could be...

i'm tired of searching for signs.
a sign to suck it up and stay.
a sign to believe this time will
be different than all the others.
a sign to further disrespect
myself by convincing my mind
that it's my fault we're failing,
that i need to do more on my end.
i'm tired of searching for signs.
i shouldn't have to constantly
manipulate my mind to forgive
you, to stay or to fight for us.
me loving you should be a big
enough sign and it's not the case.
i'm tired of searching for signs.
i think the fact that i feel like i
have to find a sign to stay is
all more reason why this cant
continue any longer.

no more chasing signs...

I believe you're sorry. I believe you when you say if you could go back in time and do it differently, you'd do it in a heartbeat. I believe you, but there are just some mistakes you make in this lifetime that can't be taken back, can't be forgotten and can't be fixed. Despite how much work, effort and how apologetic you are, there are some mistakes unfortunately you have no choice but to live with forever. I don't want you to punish yourself for it though. Mistakes are a part of life, and although there's no repairing what you broke between you and me. You now get the chance to ensure you never make a mistake of that magnitude ever again. I will forever serve as your reminder, and now if or when a situation like this ever arrives again. You'll know what's at stake, and you'll know how to prevent it. You'll be better equipped to handle it.

Your forever reminder.

you're off the hook,
you can walk away
now and I won't hold
any resentment towards
you. I won't harbor any
anger towards you. I
get it. sometimes you're
just not ready. so, I'm
giving you the opportunity
now to walk away with no
ties to me anymore. I'm
giving you an out, take it.

<u>nights like these.</u>
I'm exhausted with the
burdens I carry. I've had
enough of trying to be strong
while the weight of the world
is weighing me down and
I'm forcing myself to smile
and to be okay. that's what
everyone tells me to do. I can't
let anyone see me fall or even
look as if I'm on the verge
of throwing in the towel
because I should be happy
that I woke up this morning
when someone else didn't get
to. never being allowed to
feel anything outside of
happiness and gratitude for life,
that's what's killing me slowly.
then nights like these hit, and
all I want to do is not live so
I don't feel guilty for not being
okay. I wish they knew that
sometimes I need to fall apart
to piece myself back together
and it doesn't make me ungrateful.
I hate that nights like these exist.

I wish there was a right way to break someone's heart, a right way to walk away from someone you love, a right way to end things without any pain, heartache or anger, but there isn't. There's no right way or time to say goodbye. You just rip the band aid off and hope that outside of the pain they're feeling right now; they're aware of your heart. They know that despite the decision you made to walk away that it wasn't easy for you. You hope they understand that your choice to leave wasn't because you didn't love them, but the complete opposite in fact. It's because you do love them that you're doing what's best for the both of you even if they don't understand it yet.

A right way to say goodbye...

My love hasn't been keeping us stable.
I thought if we built our foundation
strictly off of love we'd never break.
I assumed love was that powerful
till I met you and you demolished
everything I thought I knew.

I know nothing...

she's tired of having to
wipe my tears away
because I won't let you
go. she's disappointed in
me for how long I've
allowed this to continue
but she loves me, so she
stays and she supports me.
but I can see that she's
growing weary of my lack
of self-love and self-respect.

my friend is tired...

thank you for seeing my
worth when I couldn't see.
thank you for believing in
me when I struggled with
constantly doubting myself.
thank you for never giving
up on me when I gave up on
myself countless times.
thank you for having faith in
me when I couldn't see the
light in the darkness.

to the one who loved me when I didn't deserve it.

I have to stop allowing those days where confusion, fear or disappointment strikes to overshadow how far I've come.

you want to know
how I knew we
weren't going to
make it in each
other's futures?
because in all the
time we spent
together, I never
felt happier than
when I wasn't in
your arms and I
never seen you
shine brighter than
when you weren't
in my arms.

The inevitable...

So, you miss the old me now huh? You want the old me to come back. It's mind blowing in fact because you miss a version of me that you hated. You didn't like me, you settled for me, and you were never afraid to make it known. You don't miss how I loved you, because you'd do everything in your power to escape me. You didn't miss me because you never stuck around long enough to love me in order to miss me. You can't miss the times we spent together because you'd spend the entire time telling me how I wasn't good enough. So, I'm just trying to understand how you could miss the old me unless, you miss the old me in terms of how I didn't love myself. That'd make more sense. You miss what you used to be able to get away with. You miss how weak I was and how much power I gave the words you'd use to talk down on me. You miss the old me because she didn't understand her strength or her power. You miss not having to be held accountable. You miss the control you had over me, and now that's gone there's an emptiness inside of you. Imagine that, having to drain and exhaust someone of everything to feel whole. How miserable.

You're missing the old me...

You painted your lies so beautifully
on your canvas of lies.
"I love you; I could never hurt you."
then the hurt came.
"You're so beautiful; I see no one but you."
then you saw not one, but two.
"You're my everything; she meant nothing."
yet she meant enough for you to sacrifice us.
The lies so beautiful, knowing better,
I still believed them every single time.

Your beautiful lies...

i'm in good hands now, love.
and he's nothing like you,
don't stress yourself anymore.
i'm happy
stop calling...

Do I ever cross your mind anymore? Do you ever look back at what we shared and regret what you did? Do you ever wish you could go back and do things differently? I don't know... I just wonder at times if you cared enough about me to miss me. Maybe you know the damage you caused is irreversible, so you don't bother at all to check in or even apologize. I have no idea why I'm here or why I care or why I even asked. I just... it's something that crosses my mind from time to time.

Do you ever miss me?

I wish I could've been there for you.
I feel like that's where we became at
odds and we were never able to recover
from it. I could never be there for you
the way you needed me to be and I
promise tried. I tried everything to be
what you needed while you were
struggling and I think you held it against
me the fact that I wasn't able to provide you
support in the way you needed it.
Just know there wasn't a time that I
didn't care or that I didn't beat myself
up for not understanding how to be
there for you. I'm sorry you felt alone.

I wanted to be there for you...

once you've shattered a
heart into a million pieces,
once you've broken the
trust that was built,
once the foundation
has collapsed underneath,
once you've ruined the
way they've viewed you,
and you become a stranger
they can't recognize anymore,
once you've made mistakes
repeatedly at their expense,
once you become a danger
to their idea of love.
it's too late.
there's no coming back from
that; not healthy, not happy,
and certainly not whole.

It's too late.

[15 missed calls...]

I need you to stop calling me. I can see you're sorry for the pain you've cause, and I appreciate you reaching out to me to apologize for it. It's refreshing to know that you've grown enough to recognize your faults, but you don't get to do this. You don't get to try to guilt me into coming back to you. Things can't go back to the way they used to be because what we had is broken beyond repair. I realize you were young, and you made mistakes you want to fix - but there is no fixing this and I hate to be that person, but I don't love you anymore so even if I wanted to come back, I couldn't. I didn't want to have to be this direct, but you're not my problem anymore. You don't get to act like I didn't give you all of me. Don't act blind to the fact that I gave you a million chances to change and you weren't interested. You have regrets and I know you're trying to redeem yourself. So, I do forgive you for everything, and I hope that provides some peace for you. But I'm not coming back to you.

i was your everything.
i was more than just a
girlfriend or a friend to
you. i held you together.
i was your heartbeat. you
don't want to have to do
life without me. you don't
want to let this go. i mean
too much to you.

everything you were aware of
prior to lying down with another
woman that wasn't me.

and if you could do that to
someone you call your
everything, to someone
who supposedly means
so much to you, there is no
hope for you and i to continue.

cheaters baggage.

you took me for granted
and the price you'll pay for that,
losing me and never getting the
opportunity to fix it or change
the way you mishandled me.
will haunt you forever.

you want to know if he’s treating me right? you want to know if he’s loving me the way I deserve to be? you want to know if he’s respecting me and not toying with my emotions the way you did? ultimately you want to know if I devalued myself even more than when I was with you and found someone worse than who you were to me. I don’t owe you an answer.

devalued.

mommy.
my heart in human form.
my soul in human form.
I love you is too basic
and almost disgraceful.
there are no words to
describe your impact.
there aren't enough
words to explain the
infinite love I have for
you. knowing my heart
beats only because of
you. not knowing a world
without you. you are the
sun, the moon, the stars.
the ocean, the earth.
m y e v e r y t h i n g.
thank you for loving me.

we break up and then make up
just to break up and then make up
tears fucking up my make up.
fuck that,
who's that
calling you so late?
is there somewhere else
you'd rather be?
don't bother answering
with whatever bullshit lie
that's about to spew from your lips
tired doesn't even begin to describe you.
holding you down
hasn't done shit
but break me down.
here comes another break up,
but this time won't be no make up.
you're not worth this out of me.
break up, make up with another bitch.

Break up, make up, break up, make up.

you didn't mean to hurt me,
but here we are,
and now i'm a shell of the woman i once was.
you didn't mean to make me cry,
but here we are,
and my tears have been the only consistent part
of our relationship.
you didn't mean to break my heart,
but here we are
and the pieces of my heart are shattered to the
where i'll never be able to be whole again.

you not meaning to
doesn't take away the fact that you did.
it doesn't change the pain,
it doesn't change the heartache.
in fact, it's insulting to not do anything to prevent
hurting me and yet claim that you didn't mean to.
you mean, you didn't make an effort not to.

you didn't mean to hurt me, but you did.
repeatedly.
you didn't mean to make me cry, but you did.
constantly.
you didn't mean to break my heart, but you did.
with no remorse.

truth is, you meant to.

it's time to give my heart a break.
a permanent break from inconsistent
people, from loving the wrong people,
from people who take and take, but
never look to give, from people who
don't appreciate how hard I love when
I love, from people who look to me as
someone they can run to when it's
convenient for them, from people who
don't value me, from people who don't
care about me, from people who make
me feel as if being myself isn't enough,
from people who don't deserve me. my
heart has been overworked so, we're
both done.

a heart break.

i aspire to complete
someone the way
you've completed me.

MEDICINE.

I don't want to be your medicine. The one you look for when you need to feel better, to take your pain away or to have your ego to boosted. Medicine isn't forever. Once it's done its job you don't look for it anymore, you don't prioritize it anymore, and you don't care about it anymore. I can't continue to be the one you search for when you're in need, but when you're okay; I don't get to experience that version of you. I won't be yours or anyone's medicine, never again.

teaching myself it's okay
to separate myself from
people who make it my
only option in order
to have my peace.

hope.

hoping things change.
hoping you'll love me back one day.
hoping everything will fall into place.
hoping you'll care the way I do.
hoping the darkness doesn't last forever.
hope. hope. hope. hope. hope. hope. hope.
hoping is disappointing me.
hoping is slowly killing me.
yet I still find myself holding on to it with my last breath.

when they know you love
them so much they begin
to assume you'll never
leave no matter how bad it
gets. so, they'll test you.
they'll do something small,
almost insignificant to see
how you'll react and once
you give them the green
light by not having or
enforcing consequences.
for hurting you, they'll
start to get comfortable in
knowing you'll never put
your heart through the
pain of having to walk
away from them. cocky
they start disrespecting
you, making a fool out of
you, lying to you and
dimming your light so you
don't ever get the strength
to let them go. you've realized
too late that they've taken your
love for granted. don't let
it get this far.

loving too much...

you want to leave, but you
don't want to feel at fault
for this relationship failing.
you don't want to carry that
guilt so you stay with them.
miserable, unhappy and no
peace whatsoever, but it
means you're fighting for
love right? but deep down in
your heart you know there's
no happy ending when you
choose someone over your
peace of mind and happiness.

no happy ending...

i can't fault you for not loving
me the way i needed to be loved,
i have to fault myself for hoping
one day you'd prioritize and
attempt to love me the way i've
loved you.

i apologize to myself for that.

Being disrespected, lied to, and mistreated isn't normal. And the only reason you feel like it's normal or okay is because you love this person so much, you're letting it slide. Or maybe it's because you've witnessed all throughout your life that's what love is supposed to be. Either way you begin playing the fool and playing small because you're terrified of the thought of losing them. So, unaware and unintentionally you've made the decision to choose them over you. To choose what they want and what they need or how they feel over yourself. The price for that is unimaginable. Losing yourself for love is the most dangerous thing you can do because you risk never finding yourself again. You risk seeking for love in everyone outside of yourself and not caring what the cost is. All because you loved someone so much you were willing to sacrifice yourself in the name of love. Now you don't have love and you don't have yourself.

The price of losing yourself for love.

You teach people how to treat you by what you allow them to continue and get away with.

i love people who create that
safe space for you where you
can lie all your worries and all
your expectations on the floor
like a taking your jacket off
after a long day or even better,
your bra. a safe place where
you don't feel the need to
protect yourself anymore,
you don't have to constantly
be on the lookout or waiting
for the other shoe to drop.
where you can lie your guard
down and take off the mask
you put on when you're out
in the world. where you don't
have to be pretend you're okay.
it's like their an escape from the
world. if you're fortunate enough
to find someone or something
that provides this feeling for
you, cherish it or them. they
don't come around so often.

this is my safe place.

Toxic.

They don't always come in angry, hateful, or envious. There are times where the red flags aren't as apparent and clear as people make it seem. Sometimes they come in charming, and they sweep you off your feet. You fall for it and get to a point where you're confident that they'd never hurt you. At least not intentionally so, you let everything slide. You sweep everything under the rug because there's no way this sweet, charming, loving person could ever be harmful or hurtful to you. Sometimes they've been a part of your life for so long you've become immune to the signs. It's become normal to you. "That's just the way they are." They're family or best friends since childhood or even a partner you've been in a relationship with for such a long period of time. Other times it's them constantly reassuring you that they love you more than anything in the world and they'd rather die than be without you, but it's only ever after they hurt you. There are times where they come as, "How dare you play victim when I hurt you? How dare you try to make me take accountability for hurting you? Yes, I hurt you, but I'm the victim here can't you see?" They do it so well you start questioning if you should be upset about something that clearly hurt you. Toxic people are dangerous for a reason. Manipulative, vindictive, loving, caring, gas lighter, charming, and sweet with a victim mentality, etc.

Don't make me have to be the selfish one here. You don't get to make decisions that affect the both of us and try to manipulate me into thinking I'm wrong for doing what's best for me. You don't get to decide how I should react because it might not align with your desires. I'll be the selfish one if I need to be. Someone has to look out for my best interest even if it's not ideal or what I want.

I might not ever get that everlasting fairytale love from the story books I always envisioned for myself. I really might not ever get it. I spent so much of being young preparing myself to receive that love. And I'm sitting here and it's hitting me that I might not ever get it. I figured I'd feel this infinite amount of sadness or guilt on my end for coming to this conclusion, but I don't. It's weird but I feel relief. I no longer carry the weight of expectations. I can breathe and enjoy life for what it is. I can enjoy people for who they are instead of what I'm expecting or hoping them to be or contribute to my life. Because I'm okay, either way. I've accepted I might never get that happy ever after and I'm okay. And if a miracle happens where I get that happy ever after, I'm okay with that too. But it feels liberating to remove that weight off my chest, simply by accepting that what I want or wished for may not come true.

I'm okay, either way, I'm okay.

stop seeking perfection,
start seeking authenticity.
perfection is false, it's not
real and it's not attainable.
you're asking to be fooled.
but authenticity it's real,
it's genuine, and it's honest.
you're asking for sincerity.

seek the truth.

to see all that everyone is willing
to sacrifice and give for love is
almost intimidating, alarming, and
scary. lying for love. making excuses
for love. accepting the bare minimum
for love. tolerating pain and abuse for
love. bleeding for love. losing themselves
for love. compromising their values and
morals for love. putting their mental health
at stake for love. sacrificing core beliefs
and core parts of themselves for love.
killing themselves for love. breaking their
own hearts for love. that's frightening to
know when you're in a space of searching
to love and to be loved back. i assume this
is what they mean when they say love can
be a very dangerous game to play.

all in the name of love...

I want a love that allows me to
unapologetically use my voice.
a love that understands that I
have a story to tell and it won't
always be beautiful or perfect,
but it's my truth. it deserves to
be told and heard. a love that
doesn't hinder my growth because
my light shines too damn bright
to appease their ego. a love that
contributes to my strength instead
of subtracting from it. a love that
makes my heart feel whole.

a love I yearn for.

if it was a choice i wouldn't
have chosen to love you.
to this day, even after all
that's transpired, i wouldn't
have chosen to love you.

in all actuality, i hate the
day i ever laid eyes on you
to fall in love with you. no
good came from me ever
falling in love with you.

the lessons, the message,
the reason you entered my
life was not worth a half of
the pain i endured in your
hands. you were the devil.

a demon in human form,
using your charm and smile
to latch your teeth into your
victims. make them love you
and feed off them to live.

no amount of time will ever
go by where i forgive you
for the trauma you've inflicted
onto me. loving you wasn't a
choice because who the hell
would choose this type of love?

there are just somethings
we never really heal from.
we wake up one day and
we move forward. we
carry certain situations
around with us for the rest of
our lives and we do everything
in our power to prevent it
from happening again. but
to say times heals, well i'll be
honest, it's complete bullshit.
life goes on and eventually,
after the tears, the sadness,
the grief, and the aching,
you just have to go with it.

time healing bullshit...

you'll look back and regret
a ton of things in this life,
wishing you would've said
something to that guy, wishing
you would've said i love you
sooner or wishing you never
sent it in that drunk text,
wishing you would've made
smarter choices, wishing you
would've trusted that gut feeling,
but you never regret standing
up for yourself, fighting for your
worth and using your voice.

regrets.

4. a.m. thoughts

death is so inconsiderate.
what about my plans?
what about the people who need me?
what about my life?
what about the hearts of people I've captivated?
what about the souls I have yet to experience?
why are you so inconsiderate?

<u>the girl of your dreams.</u>
i won't always agree with
you. i'm stubborn sometimes.
passionate about the things
that matters the most to me.
i'm vocal about how i feel
because my feelings deserve
to be heard and understood.
sometimes when i feel
misunderstood i run and i'm
still trying to figure out why
i do that. my laugh isn't the
cutest perfect laugh, sometimes
i laugh so hard you'd think i was
a guy. promises mean everything
to me, it's like a verbal contract to
me. i love dancing wild to my
favorite songs and singing louder
to the heartbreak songs that have
nothing to do with my life. i'm not
perfect. i have flaws and a lot of
healing to do, but this is who i
am, unapologetically. and to you
this might not mean anything, but
to the one, i'm the girl of his dreams.
to me, i'm the girl of my dreams.
and i'm more than content with that.

i knew throughout our
relationship we'd go
through normal changes,
changes to how we act
changes to how we feel
changes to how we love,
but i never thought i'd see
the day where the way
you once looked at me
would change.

you used to look at me as
if being with me meant you
had the entire world in your
vision, in your arms.

now you look at me as if i'm
someone you're going through
the motions with. someone you're
clearly not in love with anymore.

now you see right through me.

changes...

oh, how i meant so much to you,
yet you threw it all away for a
self-loathing, insecure, wanna be me bimbo.
what a shame, what a waste, what a L.

"i'm not in love with you anymore" he said,

i paused.
took a breath.
looked around at the life we built together.
attempted to hold my laugh in.

he looks at me puzzled.
probably thinks i'm going crazy,
"did you hear what i just said?"

i turn my attention to him.
feeling all the weight lifted off my heart.
i sigh in relief

"i'm not in love with you anymore either." i
laughed.

respect
all she's searching for
is respect from you.

settle the score.

give me a knife, let me carve my
name in your heart and watch you
bleed out to decide if you've earned
and are worthy of my love.

give me your head, let me hold it in
the ocean till you feel you can't breathe
any longer and i'll pull you up simply out
of obligation.

give me your legs, let me pin them down
on the side of the road, run them over with my
car back and forth, back and forth, inflicting
great pain, apologize, tell you i love you,
watch you sigh in relief, put your guard down,
and get back in my car and do it all over again.

all the torment i've suffered at your hands,
this is the smallest taste of what you put me
through. that's a glimpse of what it's like being
loved by you.

so, let's do it.
let's even the score.

i should be healing
instead, i find myself
falling in love with
you. abandoning all
the work i put in to
ensure a steady,
happy, healed future
for myself.

"reach out to me, if you're struggling."

it's kind to know you'd be here
if i ever needed you, and that
you're telling me to call you if
i need you but it doesn't change
how much of a burden i feel
reaching out to you. it's not
because of you or anything you've
done. it's me. it's all me, pounding
in my head that you've got bigger,
more serious problems to worry
about than little old me who can't
seem to shake this feeling of
darkness off, little old me who feels
so alone and cold, despite how many
people around me that love me to death.
not wanting to bring my dark clouds
over your head plays a role as well.
if i could stop feeling so useless,
so broken, so damaged, so alone, i
would. nothing brings more sadness
to my heart than knowing i can't be
who the people i love need me to be.
just add more weight to my already
heavy heart. it's not your fault, but
i can't take this anymore.

an apology that searches for sympathy
rather than taking accountability,
an apology that protests repercussions
rather than understanding the effects of their actions,
an apology aimed in placing blame elsewhere
rather than accepting there could've been fault on their end,
is not an apology worth conversating further about,
let alone accept.

apologize like you mean it.

<u>Homewrecker times two.</u>
You've broken into my home,
But you were only one of the two intruders.
You couldn't have possibly done this alone.
The other intruder lies asleep beside me.
He's created this fantasy and gave you the keys
Attempting to escape his responsibilities and reality.
You're fun, spunky, new, exciting.
It's like receiving a brand-new toy after playing with the same toy for months or years on end.
I can't even begin to imagine the lies he's told you.
So young, naïve and in love, you believe in him.
You trust him.
You've fallen for his charm, that I can't blame you for.
It's the very reason I fell for him myself.
Whether you were aware of me prior to meeting him or not,
At some point, you've questioned or come to the realization of my position.
You created a home inside of my home.
You're relying solely on the foundation that he and I created.
A foundation clearly so broken that instead of fighting to make it work, he searched elsewhere to be fulfilled.

The issue now is that you've gotten comfortable in a position that was never yours or that was never rightfully given to you.
You've gotten comfortable in a position only someone who's lacking self-worth and self-love would not only stay in but claim proudly.
You think you could never be me.
You believe you have his heart in a way I never could.
It's different with you right?
It's amusing and quite frankly entertaining to say the least.
You want this position so badly,
You're willing to compromise your self-respect and morals for it.
It's yours.
I know I make my position look effortless, happy, and fulfilling.
But that's not the half of it.
I just hope you're sympathetic and understanding to the next sparkly toy he finds after you.
Be careful what you ask for because you just might get it.
So, congrats,
Homewrecker.

i want you.
i want you.
i want you.

you don't know me.
you don't like me.
you don't value me.

you wouldn't know what to do with me.

When do you stick by someone's side while they're going through a rough patch and when do you walk away?

It's a tough question to answer because there are so many factors to it. Rough patches can range from depression, mental health issues, grieving, getting laid off at work, an injury, and so much more. I believe balance is the answer to everything in this world. There's life and there's death. There's good and there's bad. There's hell and there's heaven. In this situation, I believe a balance of compassion and boundaries are necessary.

Time qualifies as compassion. Give people the time to heal, to grieve, to get better, to want to get better, and a chance to not be okay. No one handles every situation the same but given the time to process your emotions is impactful to getting pass a rough patch.

Effort qualifies as boundaries. You can only take and deal with so much till it becomes detrimental to you. After you've provided compassion, effort needs to follow behind. Effort in healing, in grieving, and in working to better is needed for both sides. They need effort to get out of the rough patch and you need to see effort to show as light in the darkness.

Knowing yourself comes handy in so many parts of life. Ultimately you have to decide what you can handle and what you can't. You have to know when enough is enough. It's important to be there for the people you love, but it's equally as important to make sure you're there for yourself. It's easy to get wrapped up in trying to help someone heal, grieve or get better that you forget that you need to be taken care of as well. And you realistically, you can only help someone as much as they want to help themselves. You can't save everyone, you can't heal for people, and you can't grieve for them. You have to make the executive decision factoring in all of the factors.

So, when do you stick by someone's side while they're going through a rough patch and when do you walk away? Only you can answer that question but walking away needs to be the answer when it gets to a point where it's detrimental to you.

Thank you so much for buying and supporting me. Nothing means more to me than knowing my work impacted you so much that you wanted to share it with the world, your world.
All I ask is to be tagged in any of my work you post on social media.

Twitter: @Spicebae_
Instagram: @MartineAshleyS / @MartineAshleyPoetry
TikTok: @MartineAshleyPoetry
Facebook: /ReadMartineAshleyS

Thank you again for loving my work.

Check out my other books if you haven't already on the next page...

MORE FROM THIS AUTHOR.

Through The Storm is the debut book for this author. Heartbreak, pain and healing have never been tackled in the way this author tackled the subjects. In the most truthful and raw writing, the author resonates with readers from around the world who have experience heartbreak. The perfect book to make you feel less alone as you maneuver through the phases.

Aftermath is the follow up after the debut of Through The Storm. Still very much discussing topics such as heartbreak, pain and healing, now we discuss the aftermath of those subjects. Learning to how to move forward, acknowledging the roles you may have played and the red flags you might've ignored. Still carrying her truthful and raw writing. You feel as if it's your best friend speaking to you.

I Won't Apologize For What I'm About To Say is the third book from this author. This time she's done being apologetic and fitting in the lines. Still discussing topics such as heartbreak, pain, healing, death, friendship, and so much more, but this time she's not biting her tongue on these feelings she's kept inside for so long. Very much still carrying her truthful and raw writing.

Manufactured by Amazon.ca
Acheson, AB